# portfolio collection
# Helen Lancaster

**TELOS**

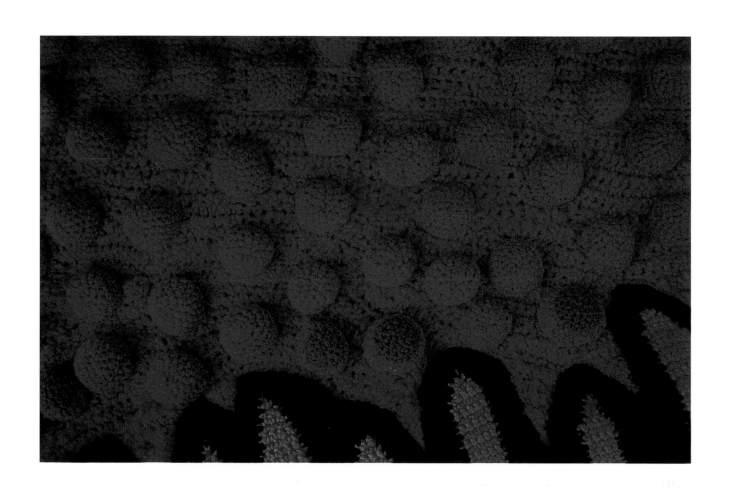

**Garibaldi**
(detail from **Celebration**)
1999
crochet
76 x 91cm (30in variable x 3ft)

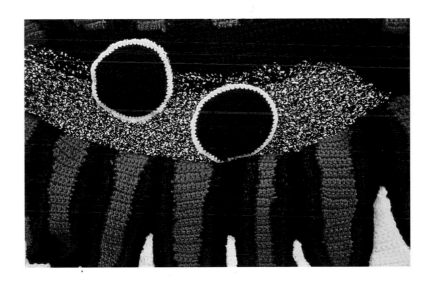

Spider Shell with Shrimp Crab
detail from **Celebration**
1999

Author: Carolynne Skinner
Project Manager: Karen Fail
Series Editor: Matthew Koumis
Reprographics: Ermanno Beverari
Printed by Grafiche AZ, Italy

**© Telos Art Publishing 2002**

Telos Art Publishing
PO Box 125, Winchester
SO23 7UJ England
T  +44 (0) 1962 864546
F  +44 (0) 1962 864727
E  editorial@telos.net
W  www.arttextiles.com

ISBN 1-902015-29-0 (softback)
ISBN 1-902015-45-2 (hardback)

A CIP catalogue record for this book
is available from the British Library

**Photo Credits**
Craig Potton: 'Barrier Reef'
(Wearable Art)
Paul Henderson Kelly: 'Barrier Reef
Surprise', 'Anchors Away', 'Coral
Flow', 'Weathered Wood III'
Eardley Lancaster:  All other photos

**Artist's Acknowledgements**
This book is dedicated to my husband
Eardley and loving family.

Special thanks to Patricia Black,
Kristen Dibbs, Karen Fail, Paul
Henderson Kelly, Susan Hutchinson,
Alice Kettle, Shirley McKernan,
Craig Potton and Carolynne Skinner.

The photo on page 13 is reproduced
with the permission of Tourism
Queensland.

**Notes**
All dimensions are shown in metric
and imperial, height x width x depth.

# Contents

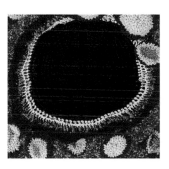

**Coral Grouper**
detail from **Celebration**
1999

# Biography

**Born**      1936 Macksville NSW, Australia

**Education**
1954-1957     East Sydney Technical College & Sydney Teachers College
1975          Alexander Mackie College of Advanced Education, Sydney

**Professional**
1995 -        Curator, Fairfield City Museum and Gallery, Sydney
1986-1990     Lecturer, Expressive and Performing Arts, St. George CAE, Sydney
1970-1986     Lecturer, Humanities, City Art Institute, Sydney
1958-1964     Teacher, Art, Secondary Schools

**Selected Solo Exhibitions**
2000          'The Coral Forest', Whitlam Library, Cabramatta
1998          'Where Have All the Fish Gone?', Braemar Contemporary Gallery, Springwood
1994          'Blue Striped Scarf', Braemar Contemporary Gallery, Springwood
1991          'My Own Private Barrier Reef', Braemar Contemporary Gallery, Springwood
1989          Guest Artist, Australian Environmental Conference, Bowral
1985          'Birds … of a Feather', Lewers Bequest and Penrith Regional Gallery
1984          'Let's Jump Across the Creek,' Hogarth Gallery, Sydney
1984          'A Walk Along the Beach', Gallery am Graben, Vienna
1982          'A Walk Along the Beach', Lewers Bequest and Penrith Regional Gallery

**Corallite Sea Floor** (detail)
1990
twin needled embroidery, white satin
43 x 43cm (17 x 17in)

portfolio collection **helen lancaster**

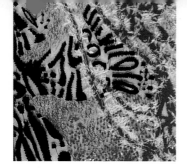

**The Barrier Reef Corporate Wall**
(detail)
1990

### Selected Group Exhibitions

| | |
|---|---|
| 2001 | Art Award, Willoughby City Civic Centre, Sydney |
| 2000 | 'The Unexpected', Fairfield City Museum & Gallery |
| 1999 | 'Hooked', Craft Queensland City Museum & Gallery (tour) |
| 1998 | 'Arts Alive University', Santo Tomas, Manila, Philippines |
| 1998 | 'Wearable Art', *NZ* Te Papa Museum, Wellington, New Zealand (tour) |
| 1998 | 'Where Have All the Fish Gone?', Great Barrier Reef Aquarium, Townsville |
| 1998 | 'International Lace Competition', Power House Museum, Sydney |
| 1997 | 'Arts Alive', Fra Angelico Gallery, Manila, Philippines |
| 1997 | Collection of Australian Textile Art toured Queensland sponsored by Bernina |
| 1996 | Guest artist, Lovett Gallery, Newcastle |
| 1996 | 'Race for a Hat', Trappings Gallery, Melbourne |
| 1996 | 'Wearable Art', *NZ* Singapore (tour) |
| 1995 | 'Australian Fashion', Framework 26 costumes, 10 pieces of artwork, Cairo, Egypt (tour) |
| 1995 | 'Arts Alive in Tourism', University of Western Sydney |
| 1995 | 'Art to Wear', City Regional Gallery, Maitland |
| 1994 | 'Art To Wear', Craftspace, Sydney |
| 1992 | 'Birds, Fish and the Environment Artists for Life', Platypus Gallery, Taronga Park Zoo, Sydney |
| 1991 | Guest artist, Celtic Foundation, Sydney University |
| 1991 | 'Camp Creative Tutors Exhibition', Grafton Regional Gallery |
| 1990 | 'National Craft Acquisition Award Exhibition', Northern Territory Museum of Arts & Sciences, Darwin |
| 1989 | 'Inside the Greenhouse', The Tin Sheds, Sydney University |
| 1989 | 'Helen Lancaster and Kristen Dibbs', Bowral Art Gallery |
| 1987 | 'Fibres and Fabrics Pacific Festival', Perc Tucker Regional Gallery, Townsville |
| 1987 | 'Innovations, Past & Present', Von Bertouch Gallery, Newcastle (catalogue) |
| 1984 | 'Arts of Oceania', Sydney Textile Museum, Mosman |
| 1984 | 'Body as a Starting Point', Gryphon Gallery, Melbourne |
| 1983 | 'Sleeping Beauty Costume and Set Design', The Australian Ballet's 21st Anniversary Competition, Sydney Opera House |

## Commissions

| | |
|---|---|
| 2000 | 'Joy of Life Shroud', Private Collection |
| 2000 | Designed Foyer Presentation for the Sydney 2000 Olympic Games, Fairfield City Council, Sydney |
| 1993 | 'Nine paintings', Forays Conference, Jupiters at Noosa |
| 1990 | 'Queen Victoria Christmas Tree Project', Crafts Council of NSW |
| 1989 | 'The Great Barrier Reef', 11 watercolours, World Headquarters, Commonwealth Bank, Sydney |
| 1989 | 'The Great Barrier Reef', 9 watercolours, State Headquarters, Commonwealth Bank, Brisbane |

## Curator, Exhibitions

(Fairfield City Museum and Gallery, Sydney, Australia)

| | |
|---|---|
| 2001 | 'Big and Bold; Small and Exquisite' 80 artists, Japanese kimonos |
| 2000 | 'It's in the Box' 60 artists, various media |
| 2000 | 'The Unexpected' 4 artists |
| 2000 | 'Surface Tension' techniques in fibre, 50 artists |
| 2000 | 'Postcards: Images of the 20th Century', 100 artists, textile postcards |
| 1999 | 'Exhibition of work by Parklands Stitchers and Newcastle Embroiderers & Textile Artists' |
| 1999 | 'Outrageous Brides' Conceptual Wearable Art, 30 artists |
| 1998 | 'Almost Somebody',102 artists, cloth doll interpretations (tour) |
| 1997 | 'The Lucky Country', ABSDA, Braemar Contemporary Gallery, Springwood |
| 1995 | '21st Birthday Celebrations for ABSDA', Arts Council Gallery, Fairfield |

**The Barrier Reef Corporate Wall**
(detail)
1990

**Community**

| | |
|---|---|
| 1991 | 'Our House', project, Rockdale Macedonian Women's Group |
| 1991 | Banner, Ethnic Communities Council of NSW (Multicultural Groups) |
| 1990 | 'Tapestry of Memories', Rockdale Macedonian Women's Group |
| 1987 | Designed Front Curtain for The Bicentennial Leycock Street Theatre, Gosford |

**Work in Public and Private Collections**

America, Vienna, Berlin, Edinburgh and Australia (Private Collections)
City Art Institute
World Headquarters, Commonwealth Bank, Sydney
State Headquarters, Commonwealth Bank, Brisbane
Headquarters, AMP and HIH Insurance Companies
Stanthorpe Regional Gallery, Queensland

**Coral Forest** (detail)
2000

# Introduction

*Soft touch environmentalism* is how artist Helen Lancaster describes her textile work. The didactics may be gentle but the message is absolutely clear. Helen sees her role as educational – showing endangered species of birds and fish and the dangers that are threatening our environment. To accentuate this message, she often uses the Great Barrier Reef as her vehicle, incorporating her interpretation of the wonders of that magical coral reef – and its denizens – which lie along the north eastern coast of Australia.

What may surprise is that Helen has not spent months or weeks or even a day diving beneath those warm waves to view first hand the source of her inspiration. Her research is painstaking and she sees the Barrier Reef as clearly in her mind's eye as she could ever see it in reality. In the series 'Where Have All the Fish Gone' (1999, ongoing), the information was based on articles from the latest scientific and marine journals. The designs for each selected topic evolved into images originally researched from photographs.

All work is supported by documentation, which is sometimes disturbing to the viewer, often confronting but always providing a talking point.

Another prominent feature of this remarkable environmentalist is her standing in the diverse community of Australian textile artists. Generosity of spirit and sharing are hallmarks of the textile community in Australia, thanks to individuals like Helen Lancaster. She is widely acknowledged as a focus for many activities, both social and formal and has been made a life member of the Australian Batik and Surface Design Association (ABSDA). Her role cannot be too highly rated as she conceives and curates original exhibitions, delivers lectures, profiles other textile artists and judges competitions. Even her critiques are highly sought after for their truthfulness and positivity.

This volume is dedicated to that component of Helen Lancaster's diverse textile art, which demonstrates her tireless work to use her textile art to raise the alarm that our delicate environment is in danger.

**Carolynne Skinner**
Arts Publisher and Gallery Director

photograph of fishes in the
Great Barrier Reef,
Queensland, Australia

The drag of chains and the
penetration of anchor
points cause massive
destruction and weakening
of the coral reef...

**Anchors Away**
from **Where Have All the Fish Gone?**
1995
machine embroidery
satin, acetate
46cm (18in) diameter

# The Woman

**Inspirations of a passionate woman**

Helen Lancaster is regularly described as a passionate woman – passionate about her work, passionate about her community of textile artists and passionate about our planet. The very profound love, which she expresses in her work, flows from the empathy she feels with nature and all humanity. *I call myself a conceptual environmentalist. The concept is of major concern. Nothing is made for its functional purpose, rather it is made for its theatricality, narrative content, to excite debate or to stimulate memory.*

She describes her work as organic. For her, the chaos in natural forms with seemingly random growth provides asymmetrical folding, layering and rhythmic manipulation. *Have you watched the gentle ebb and flow of the water, the changing patterns of light, the rhythmic movement of living forms like seaweed, anemone, fish … and loved, LOVED the sensation, the visual pleasure, the living memory?* asks Helen.

D. H. Lawrence observed that if you put life and love into the making, then more life and love will flow – through the maker and through the thing created and this is certainly true for Helen. She, like many other women textile artists, are amongst those picking up on the messages of today's prophets; people such as David Suzuki, Jacques Cousteau, Helen Caldicott and many more. Helen dedicates many of her wearable works of art or textile pieces to special or threatened creatures such as the spotted hermit crab, pelican and owls.

Soft touch environmentalism delivers the messages about the fragile beauty of the natural world through a parade of beautiful sculptured forms.

# Early Work 1980 - 1989

From 1960-1980, Helen Lancaster created hand-embroidered fantasy animals and lengths of silk-screened and block-printed fabrics, some of which were sent to America. Her first solo exhibition, 'Machine Embroidered Sculptures and other Fantasies' was held in the Chameleon Gallery, Mosman, Sydney in 1980. A large portion of the work consisted of crocheted reef forms. Some pieces were sold. From this exhibition evolved 'A Walk Along The Beach' with two more years' work added. It was shown at the Lewers Bequest and Penrith Regional Gallery, Penrith in 1982. Consisting of 76 pieces, some quite large, this exhibition had taken Helen Lancaster ten years to complete. In 1984, 36 pieces of 'A Walk Along The Beach' were shown at the Gallery am Graben, Vienna. A few pieces were purchased.

After 1984, Helen Lancaster did not crochet again until 1998 when invited to participate in the 'Hooked' exhibition, curated by Bronwin Bourke. Her work was titled 'Celebration'. In those early years the perception of textiles as an art form was not widely held, and little has changed since that time. Limited venues were available and crochet was, and still is, regarded as a home craft.

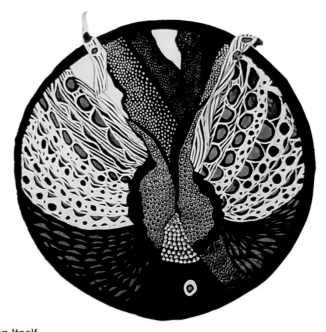

**Bird Preening Itself**
1982
machine and hand embroidery
91cm diameter (36in)

The problem of whether to frame works, making them treasured objects or leaving them unframed to allow the beauty of the textiles to be seen, remains an ongoing issue for Helen Lancaster. In 'The Walk Along the Beach', ten large machine embroidered works were framed in deep Perspex boxes to protect the three-dimensional effect created by underlying blocks of polystyrene. The forms suggested overhanging rocky ledges under which creatures hid within the shadows of the water or weather beaten rocks found along some Australian beaches. It was requested that the boxes be removed and the textiles be reframed in open mounts for the Vienna exhibition. This dilemma in framing is ongoing for Helen Lancaster. In 1998 in 'Where Have the Fish Gone', each work was stretched over a covered circle of Perspex and centred on an opaque Perspex square.

The use of reverse garbage has always intrigued Helen Lancaster and continues to do so. 'Let's Cross the Bridge' (1985 series) combined threads, linoleum tiles, pill boxes and scraps of fibre pieces combined with plastics. 'Anemone' (1989) featured cosmetic appliances with transparent plastic handles on orange pads used as centres within the crystal organza surrounds. Other spiky or hairy objects like eyelash brushes and especially plastic tops with tubing which could be combined with exotic materials, machine embroidery and fabric manipulation formed many individual pieces in 'My Own Private Barrier Reef' (1991).

The earlier period of Helen Lancaster's work generally had more subdued colouring, although reaction to some of the underwater creatures inspired a love of bright colours. These colours now dominate her current work as she has gained more confidence. The need to reflect her Australian heritage rather than follow global trends of sophistication with neutral colours has also played a part in the change. The access to photographic images in rich colour by excellent photographers occurring only in the last fifteen years has had a major impact on Helen Lancaster's choice of colour.

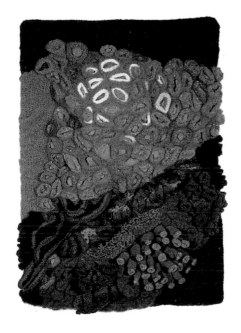

**Organic Reef in Blue**
1982
crochet
wool, mohair
122 x 92cm (48 x 36in)

Interest in spotted creatures in the early crocheted work was transferred to spotted bower birds, owls, red tailed black cockatoos, little wattle birds and other dotted birds in costumes made for 'Birds of a Feather' (1985). Spotted barks on trees resulted in 36 paintings not yet exhibited. Spots and dots have been captured in the eyes of the red spotted eel and fish in the 'Crocheted Celebration' (1999), as well as many wearable art costumes based on crabs and fish. These spots are definitely an ongoing love.

Much of the work asks to be touched. There are often hollows, cavernous areas, protuberances to poke fingers into, fluffy little balls or continuously changing textures. In the 'Walk Along the Beach' exhibition, children were encouraged to move crocheted reef pieces around to make their own personal reef. Helen Lancaster lectured to them about the shapes of the coral and the correlation between the creature's mouths and body shapes in sourcing food.

Further work will include additions to the 'Corporate Wall, Where Have All the Fish Gone?' and the 'Coral Forest'. New work envisaged will include textile sculptures titled 'Cousteau's Dream'. Whatever exploration and experimentation Helen Lancaster undertakes, it will produce new techniques and further joy to the viewer.

Let's Cross the Bridge No 4
1985
mixed media
122 x 91 x 10cm (48 x 36 x 4in)

'A Bird's Eye View' is a machine embroidery on acetate with a small amount of satin. From this gaze downward on our land, a 'Peace Statement' began to evolve: the artist was very conscious of the threat of nuclear war and the possible destruction of our entire world...

**A Bird's Eye View (Peace Statement)**
1984
machine embroidery on acetate
with satin inlay
122 x 91cm (48 x 36in)

ALL work is *in progress* …

Helen Lancaster's artworks grow organically.

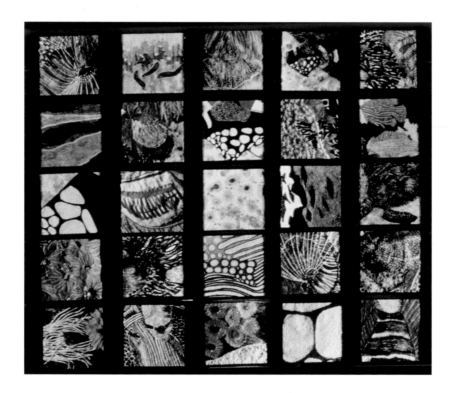

**The Barrier Reef Corporate Wall**
1990
machine embroidery on acetate
25 squares each 25cm (10in)

# The Barrier Reef Corporate Wall

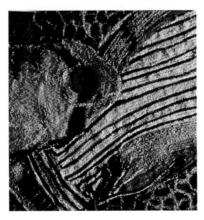

**The Barrier Reef Corporate Wall**
(details)
1990

This work is like the multiple windows in an aquarium, with kaleidoscopic glimpses of fish flashing by. 'The Barrier Reef Corporate Wall' was first exhibited in 1990 with 25 tiles and it is still growing: – it will ultimately consist of 150 tiles.

*This is a memory wall reminding me of the beauty of the Great Barrier Reef or the magical glimpses when peering under water with that first pair of goggles. I want people to love and cherish this enchanting heritage*, says Helen.

Helen works on transparent acetate to achieve the illusion of water and uses brilliant colours to create exciting colour combinations.

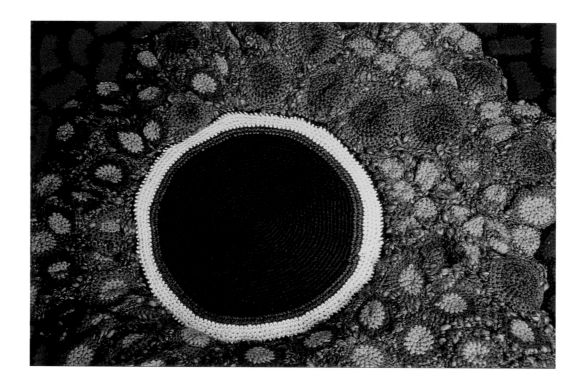

**Blue Devil**
(detail from **Celebration**)
1999

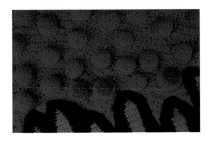

**Garibaldi**
(detail from **Celebration**)
1999

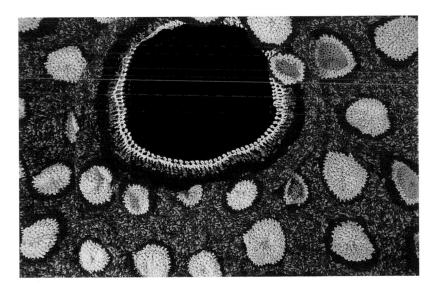

**Coral Grouper**
(detail from **Celebration**)
1999

# Celebration

'Celebration' (1999)
consists of four panels
of crochet. Vibrant colours
and beautiful abstract
shapes reveal the
distinctive eyes of the
Barrier Reef's creatures –
among them the coral
grouper, soldier fish,
moray eel and blue devil.
A myriad of dots
surrounding the eyes
simulate the Olympiad
fireworks above.

**Celebration**
1999
crochet
each panel 244 x 61 x 15cm
(96 x 144 x 6in)

# Techniques

Techniques evolve in answer to needs.

Helen Lancaster has often alternated painting exhibitions (generally water colours) with textile exhibitions. Work with fabric and thread is always intuitively created without accurate drawing or planning. She has found that detailed drawings destroy the spontaneity and freshness of her work in textiles. A few quick sketches may suggest possible directions to take but often are totally dispensed with once the work is underway.

Textural form dominates Helen Lancaster's work – and her time. *Textures bubble, collide and explode as I manipulate the fabrics into more sculptural forms.* Free machine embroidery work is produced on an 830 Bernina domestic sewing machine.

Most of Helen Lancaster's techniques are accomplished with just three stitches on her machine — the straight, zigzag and satin stitches. She enjoys changing the surface with pin tucks adjacent to each other using twin needles, shirring with elastic hand wound onto the bobbin, sewing with straight lines and shapes like O's and C's, creating dots using satin stitch and manipulating the created fabric further with padding. One of her favourite special effects is obtained by satin stitching over and over on the same line until it makes a high ridge. *I started to do this as a result of seeing a Roualt painting. It was astonishing to me to see the thickness of the dark outline around the colour. Although I was using neutrals – brown with a white outline – I persisted, even though it was a fairly dangerous and expensive technique, given the number of needles I broke* (see 'Bird Preening Itself' p18).

In work like 'The Coral Forest' (see p40) manipulated forms are created from contrasts of matt and gloss, smooth and hairy, opaque, transparent or translucent materials. *Strong tonal and textural work labels me as an organic creature.* The sculptural forms are created in most cases by multiples or variations of a form which are based on research and observation of creatures in nature. Sometimes pattern is important and at other times it is the shape that inspires. Assemblage can be heavy and arduous. There is the exhaustion of long, often tedious hours creating millions of stitches by machine and considerable physical strength is required to handle the large pieces of weighty cloth. Many sections with multitudes of protuberances have to be sewn on by hand.

Unlike many artists, Helen Lancaster does not keep her ideas in a collectable artist's book. An incredibly large personal reference library stimulates, amazes and delights Helen Lancaster. Glimpses of worlds unseen in rain forests, wetlands, deserts and oceans are captured by photographers in detailed close-ups and Helen Lancaster's imagination translates these images into textiles that become entirely her own creations.

**Carolynne Skinner**
Arts Publisher and Gallery Director

Coral Forest (detail)
2000

Underground volcanic
forms create thermal jets
where exotic creatures live.

**Barrier Reef Surprise**
1990
machine embroidery with shirring
100 x 91 x 11cm (39 x 3 x 4in)

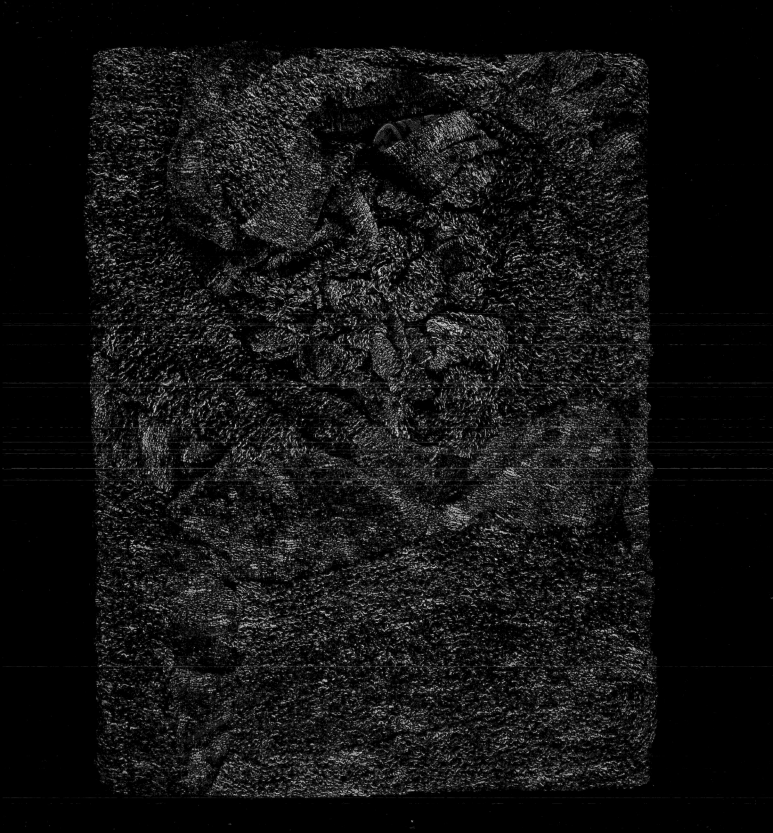

portfolio collection **helen lancaster**

# Wearable Art

Helen's aim in her prize-winning 'Barrier Reef' costume was to evoke the fragility of the precious reef environment, with coral polyps forming the garland top and coral formations the skirt. The choice of a long skirt was a reference to the early Christian missionaries' practice of requiring Pacific Islanders to wear long skirts and to refrain from swimming. The head-dress represents the poisonous scorpion fish, or zebra fish.

**Barrier Reef, Wearable Art**
1995
machine embroidered and fabric manipulated
velvet
human body dimensions

**Clustered Coral with Nudibranch**
1990
twin needling
23 x 28cm (9 x 11in)

from **Where Have All the Fish Gone?**
1995

above and right:
**Coral Forest** (detail)
2000
machine embroidery and fabric manipulation
columns range in height 107 x 310cm (42 x 120in)

'Helen in Wonderland' (2000) is an installation made up of a number of vertical poles depicting a forest of corals, a magical place where Alice in Wonderland might wander. Visitors, like Alice, explore the world of corals at the 'Barrier Reef', *swimming* between the swaying columns created from rich velvets, machine embroidery and fabrics manipulated to create 3-dimensional forms. Large textures have been miniaturized to achieve a special effect, while others have been enlarged. Today, what began as 'Helen in Wonderland' has gradually evolved into the 'Coral Forest', an installation of 20 columns.

above and right:
**Coral Forest** (details)
2000
machine embroidery and fabric manipulation
columns range in height 107 x 310cm (42 x 120in)

**Coral Flow**
2001
machine embroidered, twin needled velvet
61 x 51 x 10cm (24 x 20 x 4in)

portfolio collection **helen lancaster**

**Crown of Thorns, Anemones & Clown Fish** (detail)
1995
hand drawing on satin
242 x 112cm (90 x 44in)

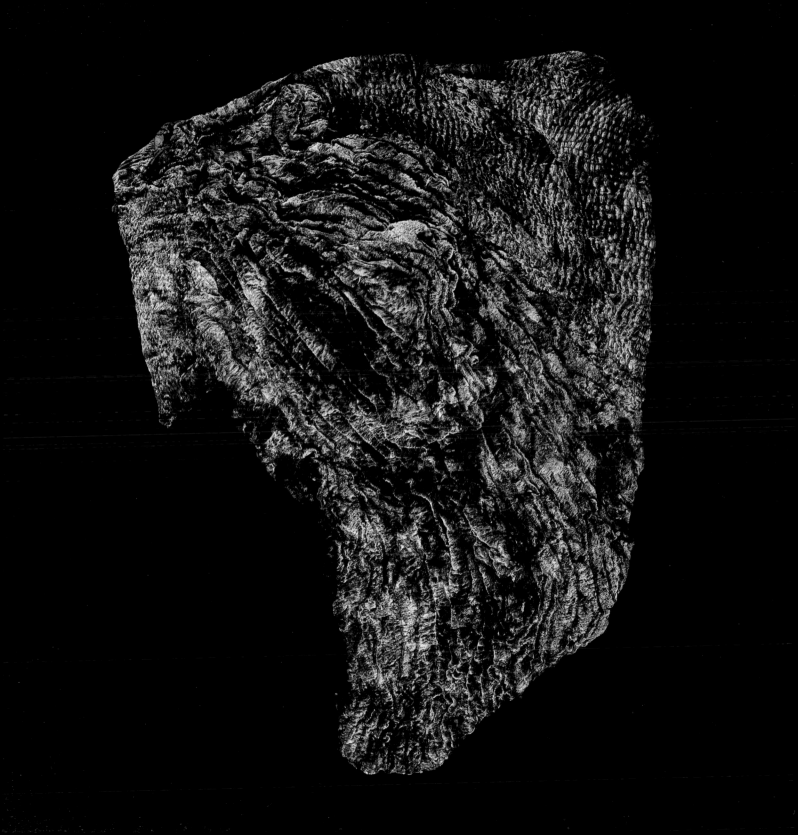

# Other titles in this series

### Vol 6: Anne Wilson
by Tim Porges and Hattie Gordon
This important American artist uses human hair, table linens and hand-stitching to probe poignant personal memories and histories, as well as evoking a subtle sense of landscape.
ISBN 1 902015 22 3 (softback)

### Vol 11: Marian Smit (April 2002)
by Marjolein v.d. Stoep
1st Prize winner in Third International Paper Triennal, Switzerland, 1999. "Work of great simplicity combining technique and poetry."
ISBN 1 902015 32 0 (softback)
ISBN 1 902015 46 0 (hardback)

### Vol 7: Alice Kettle (February 2003)
by Dr Jennifer Harris
Get up close and intimate with recent major works by this Winchester-based painter who has become one of the world's most popular embroiderers.
ISBN 1 902015 31 2 (softback)
ISBN 1 902015 53 3 (hardback)

### Vol 12: Chiyoko Tanaka (April 2002)
by Lesley Millar
Tanaka's prized weavings are in public collections around the world. A leading light from Kyoto, her work is breathtaking and awe-inspiring.
ISBN 1 902015 24 X (softback)
ISBN 1 902015 42 8 (hardback)

### Vol 8: Helen Lancaster (April 2002)
by Carolynne Skinner
The perilous fragility of nature, beautifully depicted by an outstanding conceptual environmentalist using paint, crochet, embroidery and fabric manipulation.
ISBN 1 902015 29 0 (softback)
ISBN 1 902015 45 2 (hardback)

### Volume 14: Lia Cook (September 2002)
by Jenni Sorkin
Lia Cook's provocative weavings combine aspects of digital technology, painting and photography. Referencing diverse art histories, her images are distilled from a seemingly random movement of threads.
ISBN 1 902015 34 7 (softback)
ISBN 1 902015 51 7 (hardback)

### Vol 9: Kay Lawrence (April 2002)
by Dr Diana Wood Conroy
One of the world's top tapestry weavers, her recent work negotiates issues about identity in textures ranging from minimal to lush, from sensuous to spiky.
ISBN 1 902015 28 2 (softback)
ISBN 1 902015 44 4 (hardback)

### Volume 15: Jane Lackey (September 2002)
by Irena Hofmann and Helga Pakasaar
Artist-in-residence at Cranbrook Academy of Art, her sculptural objects, installations and prints offer beguiling contemplations on the patterns, codes and maps of information concealed within the body.
ISBN 1 902015 35 5 (softback)
ISBN 1 902515 52 5 (hardback)

### Vol 10: Joan Livingstone (April 2002)
by Gerry Craig
Livingstone's powerful installations incorporate felt, stitch and epoxy resin. Professor of Fiber and Material Studies in Chicago, she is one of America's most important sculptors.
ISBN 1 902015 27 4 (softback)
ISBN 1 902015 43 6 (hardback)

**Please visit our website for details of all other volumes in this growing series.**
**www.arttextiles.com**

**Weathered Wood II**

2001

machine embroidery and fabric manipulation

size of small piece of wood

**Weathered Wood III**

2001

shirred dyed velvet fabric manipulation

79 x 74 x 20cm (31 x 22 x 8in)